Ashtanga Hridayam, Sutrasthana

(Chapter 2)

Dinacharya

By

Raju Raval

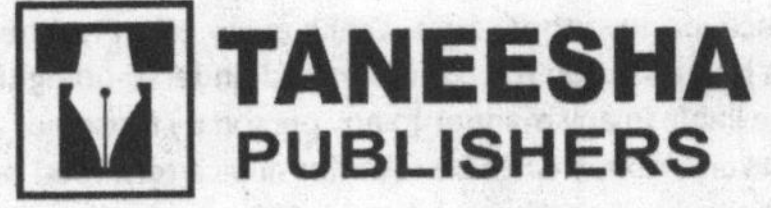

Title   : Ashtanga Hridayam, Sutrasthana (Chapter 2)

Author   : Raju Raval

Edition : First (December, 2024)

ISBN   : 9789348037091

Published by

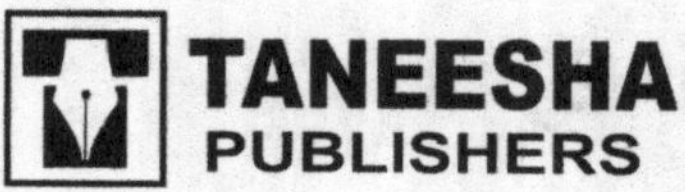

TANEESHA PUBLISHERS | *A Venture by -*
PRACHI DIGITAL PUBLICATION

Regd. Add.: 254, Khuriyakhatta No. 10, Bindukhatta,
Lalkuan, Nainital - 262402, Uttarakhand, India
Website : www.taneeshapublishers.in
E-mail : taneeshapublishers@gmail.com
Phone : +91 8454 812712, +91 8057 812712

Printed by :

Manipal Technologies Limited, Bengaluru - 560001, Karnataka

Highlights of Chapter 2: *Dinacharya* (Daily Routine)

from the *Ashtanga Hridayam*, Sutrasthana:

1. Importance of Daily Routine (Dinacharya):

- The chapter emphasizes the need for a structured daily routine to maintain balance among the three Doshas (*Vata*, *Pitta*, *Kapha*), enhance immunity (*Ojas*), and promote physical, mental, and spiritual well-being.
- Aligning daily activities with nature's rhythms helps maintain harmony with the circadian cycle.

2. Waking Up During *Brahma Muhurta*

- **Time:** Approximately 90 minutes before sunrise.
- **Purpose:** Ideal for spiritual practices, meditation, and preparing the mind and body for the day. It supports mental clarity, calmness, and enhances energy levels.

3. Oral Hygiene and Cleansing Practices:

- **Tongue Scraping:** Removes toxins (*Ama*), enhances taste perception, and aids digestion.
- **Brushing Teeth:** Use herbal twigs like *Neem* or *Licorice* for healthy teeth and gums.
- **Gargling (Kavala/Gandusha):** Using oil or herbal decoctions strengthens teeth, prevents bad breath, and clears toxins from the oral cavity.

4. Nasya (Nasal Cleansing):

- Instilling medicated oils in the nostrils clears nasal passages, enhances sensory functions, and supports respiratory health.
- It is particularly beneficial for balancing *Vata* and *Kapha* in the head region.

5. Abhyanga (Oil Massage):

- A daily practice of oil massage nourishes the body, improves skin tone, relaxes muscles, and strengthens joints.
- Balances *Vata*, improves circulation, and promotes a sense of well-being.

6. Exercise (Vyayama):

- Regular exercise enhances strength, flexibility, metabolism, and digestion.
- Recommended to be performed in moderation, suitable to one's capacity, and best during early morning hours to reduce Kapha-related heaviness.

7. Bathing (Snana):

- Cleansing the body removes impurities, refreshes the mind, and balances Doshas.
- Cold water is recommended for Pitta-dominant individuals, while warm water is suitable for Vata and Kapha types.

8. Meals and Digestion:

- **Timing:** Eating meals at regular intervals ensures proper digestion and absorption.
- **Quantity:** Moderation in eating is emphasized to maintain a healthy digestive fire (*Agni*). Overeating is discouryaged as it causes *Ama* (toxins) and imbalances.
- Foods should align with the season, Dosha, and

individual constitution.

9. Sleep and Rest:

- Adequate sleep is essential for tissue repair, mental rejuvenation, and Dosha balance.
- Sleeping during the day is generally discouraged as it increases Kapha, except for specific conditions like exhaustion or during summer.

10. Meditation and Mindfulness:

- Daily meditation and mindfulness practices are recommended to calm the mind, enhance focus, and foster emotional balance.
- These practices are aligned with the holistic goal of achieving harmony between body, mind, and spirit.

11. Seasonal Variations and Flexibility:

- Adjustments in the daily routine are advised based on seasonal changes (*Ritucharya*) to adapt to the environment and prevent Dosha imbalances.

- For instance, during spring, Kapha cleansing routines are emphasized, while cooling practices are prioritized in summer.

12. Activities to Avoid:

- Sleeping immediately after meals or during the day.
- Overeating or fasting excessively.
- Avoid excessive talking, shouting, or exposure to extreme weather conditions, as these can disturb Dosha balance.

13. Spiritual Practices:

- Time in the morning is ideal for spiritual activities, such as chanting, prayer, or meditation, to align oneself with nature and improve inner harmony.

14. Key Benefits of Following Dinacharya:

- Harmonizes biological rhythms with nature.
- Prevents Dosha imbalances and diseases.
- Enhances longevity, immunity (*Ojas*), and mental

clarity.

- Improves digestion, energy levels, and emotional stability.

Chapter 2, *Dinacharya* (*Daily Routine*) from the *Ashtanga Hridayam, Sutrasthana* with relevant sutras and their explanations:

---

1. Waking Up During *Brahma Muhurta*

Sutra:

ब्राह्मे मुहूर्ते उत्तिष्ठेत् स्वस्थो रक्षार्थमायुष:॥

(*Brāhme muhūrte uttiṣṭhet svastho rakṣārtham āyuṣaḥ.*)

Translation: One should wake up during *Brahma Muhurta* (approximately 90 minutes before sunrise) to protect and enhance life span.

Explanation:

- Waking up early aligns the body with the natural circadian rhythms.

- This is the most sattvic (calm and pure) time of the day, ideal for meditation, yoga, and introspection, supporting mental clarity and spiritual growth.

---

2. Oral Hygiene

Sutra:

दन्तधावनं कुर्याद् कषायतिक्तकटुरसै:।

(*Dantadhāvanam kuryād kaṣāya-tikta-kaṭurasaḥ.*)

Translation: One should brush teeth with twigs of plants that are astringent, bitter, or pungent in taste.

Explanation:

- Herbal twigs like Neem, Babool, and Licorice are antimicrobial, prevent dental decay, and strengthen gums.

- Regular brushing removes toxins (*Ama*) and maintains oral health.

---

3. Tongue Scraping

Sutra:

जिह्वानिर्लेखनं कुर्यात् मलाद्दोषविनाशनम्॥

(*Jihvānirlēkhanam kuryāt malāddoṣavināśanam.*)

Translation: Tongue scraping should be performed to remove impurities (*Ama*) and balance the Doshas.

Explanation:

- It removes the white coating on the tongue caused by toxins, improves taste perception, and enhances digestion.

- Tongue scraping also promotes oral hygiene and prevents bad breath.

---

4. Abhyanga (Oil Massage)

Sutra:

स्निग्धशरीरोऽभ्यङ्गः कार्यः सैषः सुखायुषः।

(*Snigdhaśarīro'bhyaṅgaḥ kāryaḥ saiṣaḥ sukhāyuṣaḥ.*)

Translation: Oil massage (Abhyanga) should be performed daily, as it promotes long life, health, and happiness.

Explanation:

- Regular oil massage nourishes the skin, strengthens muscles, and improves circulation.

- It is particularly effective in balancing *Vata Dosha*, preventing dryness, and reducing stress.

---

5. Vyayama (Exercise)

Sutra:

हृष्टः स्तैत्यं लगुत्वं च व्यायामादुपजायते॥

(*Hṛṣṭaḥ staittyam laghutvam ca vyāyāmād upajāyate.*)

Translation: Exercise enhances lightness of the body, stability, and strength.

Explanation:

- Regular exercise promotes flexibility, digestion, and circulation.

- It should be done in moderation, appropriate to one's strength and season, to avoid excessive fatigue.

6. Bathing (Snana)

Sutra:

स्नानं जाङ्गल्यशरीरत्वं बलं जीवितं आयुः सुखम्॥

(*Snānaṃ jāṅgalyaśarīratvaṃ balaṃ jīvitaṃ āyuḥ sukham.*)

Translation: Bathing promotes cleanliness, strength, longevity, and happiness.

Explanation:

- Bathing removes impurities, refreshes the body and mind, and balances Doshas.

- Cold water baths are ideal for reducing Pitta, while warm water is better for Vata and Kapha individuals.

---

7. Nasya (Nasal Therapy)

Sutra:

नासिक्यं शिरसो द्वारं तेन तन्मलनिर्गमः॥

(*Nāsikyaṃ śiraso dvāraṃ tena tanmalanirgamah.*)

Translation: The nose is the gateway to the head, and nasal therapy removes impurities from this region.

Explanation:

- Nasya (applying medicated oils to the nose) clears nasal passages, enhances respiratory function, and balances Kapha and Vata Doshas.

- It also improves cognitive function and prevents disorders like headaches and sinus issues.

8. Food and Digestion

Sutra:

समं समग्रं दिनमर्धे तु भुञ्जीत।

(*Samaṃ samagraṃ dinamardhe tu bhuñjīta.*)

Translation: Meals should be taken at appropriate times in moderate quantities.

Explanation:

- Eating at regular intervals maintains the digestive fire (*Agni*).

- Overeating or irregular eating disrupts digestion and leads to the accumulation of toxins (*Ama*).

9. Sleep and Rest

Sutra:

सुखं दुःखं आयुः ह्रासः तस्मादाहारायं निद्रा।

(*Sukhaṃ duḥkhaṃ āyuḥ hrāsaḥ tasmād āhārāyaṃ nidrā.*)

Translation: Proper sleep brings happiness and longevity, while improper sleep results in unhappiness and shortened lifespan.

Explanation:

- Proper sleep is essential for tissue repair, mental

rejuvenation, and Dosha balance.

- Sleeping during the day (unless in summer or due to exhaustion) is discouraged, as it increases Kapha and causes indigestion.

10. Meditation and Spiritual Practices

Sutra:

ध्यानं चित्तप्रसादाय सुखाया।

(*Dhyānaṃ cittaprasādāya sukhāya.*)

Translation: Meditation calms the mind and brings happiness.

Explanation:

- Meditation is emphasized as a daily practice to promote inner peace, focus, and emotional balance.

- Practicing meditation during *Brahma Muhurta* enhances its benefits, as the mind is naturally calm and receptive at this time.

11. Seasonal Variations (Ritucharya)

Sutra:

कालेन नियतं कर्म स्यात् ऋतुमानसंग्रहः॥

(*Kālena niyataṃ karma syāt ṛtumāna-saṃgrahaḥ.*)

Translation: Seasonal routines should be adapted to maintain harmony with nature.

Explanation:

- Daily routines should align with seasonal changes to prevent Dosha imbalances.

- For instance, Kapha-cleansing practices are emphasized in spring, and cooling practices are prioritized in summer.

---

12. Avoiding Improper Activities

Sutra:

न च निद्रा तु दिवा सेवनीया॥

(*Na ca nidrā tu divā sevanīyā.*)

Translation: Sleeping during the day is not advised.

Explanation:

- Daytime sleep increases Kapha, slows metabolism, and causes indigestion.

- Exceptions include extreme fatigue, illness, or summer seasons where heat depletes the body's energy.

Key Benefits of Dinacharya:

Sutra:

सुखायुः स्मृतिबुद्ध्याग्निबलप्रवृत्तिकरणि दिनचर्या॥

(*Sukhāyuḥ smṛti-buddhy-agni-bala-pravṛtti-karaṇi dinacaryā.*)

Translation: A proper daily routine promotes happiness, longevity, memory, intelligence, digestion, and strength.

Explanation:

- A disciplined lifestyle keeps the body and mind in balance, preventing disease and fostering optimal health.

Multiple-choice questions (MCQs) about Chapter 2, "Dinacharya," from the *Ashtanga Hridayam*, Sutrasthana:

---

1. What does "Dinacharya" mean?

a) Daily routine

b) Seasonal routine

c) Night regimen

d) Ayurvedic herbs

Answer: a) Daily routine

---

2. According to Dinacharya, what is the best time to wake up?

a) 10:00 AM

b) Just before sunrise

c) At noon

d) At midnight

Answer: b) Just before sunrise

---

3. Which bodily waste is recommended to be expelled immediately after waking up?

a) Urine and stool

b) Sweat

c) Tears

d) Phlegm

Answer: a) Urine and stool

---

4. What is the first activity recommended after waking up?

a) Exercise

b) Meditation

c) Drinking water

d) Brushing teeth

Answer: d) Brushing teeth

---

5. What is the Ayurvedic term for tongue scraping?

a) Gandusha

b) Abhyanga

c) Jihva Nirlekhana

d) Nasya

Answer: c) Jihva Nirlekhana

---

6. Which substance is NOT traditionally recommended for tongue scraping?

a) Gold

b) Silver

c) Bamboo

d) Plastic

Answer: d) Plastic

7. What is Gandusha?

a) Oil pulling

b) Tongue scraping

c) Nasal cleansing

d) Bathing

Answer: a) Oil pulling

8. Which oil is often used for Gandusha (oil pulling)?

a) Coconut oil

b) Sesame oil

c) Olive oil

d) Mustard oil

Answer: b) Sesame oil

9. What is the purpose of applying Anjana (collyrium) to the eyes?

a) To improve digestion

b) To enhance vision

c) To clean the ears

d) To prevent hair loss

Answer: b) To enhance vision

10. Which of the following is NOT recommended for daily use as per Dinacharya?

a) Exercise

b) Head massage

c) Nasya (nasal cleansing)

d) Sleeping during the day

Answer: d) Sleeping during the day

---

11. How often should one perform Abhyanga (oil massage)?

a) Every day

b) Once a week

c) Once a month

d) Only during festivals

Answer: a) Every day

---

12. What is the benefit of Abhyanga?

a) Improves skin complexion

b) Enhances flexibility

c) Relieves fatigue

d) All of the above

Answer: d) All of the above

13. Nasya involves the application of medicine through which route?

a) Oral

b) Nasal

c) Rectal

d) Topical

Answer: b) Nasal

---

14. What is the recommended duration for exercise as per Dinacharya?

a) Until the body feels light and sweat appears

b) Until exhaustion

c) Only 5 minutes

d) No specific time is mentioned

Answer: a) Until the body feels light and sweat appears

---

15. Which of the following should NOT be done immediately after exercise?

a) Eating food

b) Taking a bath

c) Drinking a small amount of water

d) Resting briefly

Answer: a) Eating food

16. Bathing helps in:

a) Improving digestion

b) Reducing fatigue

c) Enhancing energy levels

d) All of the above

Answer: d) All of the above

17. What type of clothing is recommended after bathing?

a) Tight-fitting clothes

b) Loose and clean clothes

c) Wet clothes

d) Clothes made of synthetic fibers

Answer: b) Loose and clean clothes

18. How should meals be consumed according to Dinacharya?

a) Quickly and without focus

b) In silence, while sitting calmly

c) While walking or standing

d) Only at night

Answer: b) In silence, while sitting calmly

19. Which season is related to Kapha Dosha accumulation, requiring lighter routines?

a) Winter

b) Summer

c) Spring

d) Rainy season

Answer: a) Winter

---

20. What is the ideal time for sleeping at night as per Dinacharya?

a) Just after sunset

b) Around midnight

c) 2–3 hours after sunset

d) Early in the morning

Answer: c) 2–3 hours after sunset

---

21. Which oil is recommended for head massage to improve sleep quality?

a) Coconut oil

b) Sesame oil

c) Neem oil

d) Sandalwood oil

Answer: a) Coconut oil

22. What activity is strictly avoided during midday as per Ayurveda?

a) Eating

b) Sleeping

c) Walking

d) Drinking water

Answer: b) Sleeping

---

23. What is the main objective of following Dinacharya?

a) To treat diseases

b) To enhance spiritual practices

c) To maintain health and prevent diseases

d) To build muscles

Answer: c) To maintain health and prevent diseases

---

24. Drinking warm water in the morning is believed to:

a) Improve digestion

b) Flush out toxins

c) Promote bowel movement

d) All of the above

Answer: d) All of the above

25. Which of the following practices is specifically recommended for maintaining oral health?

a) Brushing with herbal powders

b) Using toothpicks made from medicinal twigs

c) Oil pulling

d) All of the above

Answer: d) All of the above

---

26. Which type of water is recommended for drinking in the morning as per Ayurveda?

a) Cold water

b) Warm water

c) Iced water

d) Tap water

Answer: b) Warm water

Explanation: Warm water in the morning helps stimulate digestion, supports bowel movements, and aids in the detoxification process.

---

27. What is the primary purpose of applying collyrium (Anjana) daily?

a) To beautify the eyes

b) To improve eyesight and clear the eyes

c) To reduce body heat

d) To prevent dry skin

Answer: b) To improve eyesight and clear the eyes

Explanation: Applying collyrium removes impurities, soothes the eyes, and prevents conditions like watering and redness.

---

28. What is the recommended direction for sleeping?

a) Head facing east or south

b) Head facing north

c) Head facing west

d) No specific direction

Answer: a) Head facing east or south

Explanation: Sleeping with the head to the east promotes spiritual energy and calmness, while sleeping with the head to the south supports physical well-being by aligning with Earth's magnetic field.

---

29. Why is nasal oil application (Nasya) suggested in Dinacharya?

a) To prevent dryness in the nose

b) To enhance the functioning of the senses

c) To improve memory and focus

d) All of the above

Answer: d) All of the above

Explanation: Nasya lubricates nasal passages, clears sinuses, prevents dryness, and enhances sensory perception and cognitive functions.

30. Which season requires the most attention to prevent Kapha-related imbalances?

a) Summer

b) Winter

c) Spring

d) Rainy season

Answer: c) Spring

Explanation: Kapha tends to accumulate in winter and manifests during spring, requiring measures like exercise, light diet, and reduced oil use to balance it.

---

31. Why is daily exercise emphasized in Dinacharya?

a) To burn calories

b) To enhance flexibility, strength, and digestion

c) To reduce stress

d) Both b and c

Answer: d) Both b and c

Explanation: Exercise improves muscle tone, digestion, and metabolism. It also balances Vata and reduces mental stress.

---

32. What is the primary benefit of performing oil massage (Abhyanga) daily?

a) Promotes hair growth

b) Improves skin glow and joint lubrication

c) Increases Kapha

d) Causes lethargy

Answer: b) Improves skin glow and joint lubrication

Explanation: Abhyanga nourishes the body, improves circulation, and relieves fatigue, enhancing overall physical and mental health.

---

33. What is the importance of cleaning the ears (Karna Purana)?

a) To remove dirt

b) To improve hearing ability

c) To lubricate the ear canals and prevent Vata imbalance

d) For cosmetic reasons

Answer: c) To lubricate the ear canals and prevent Vata imbalance

Explanation: Karna Purana (oil application in ears) prevents dryness, strengthens hearing, and balances Vata in the head region.

---

34. Which Dosha is primarily balanced by oil massage?

a) Vata

b) Pitta

c) Kapha

d) All of the above

Answer: a) Vata

Explanation: Abhyanga stabilizes and nourishes the body, effectively calming the dryness and restlessness caused by aggravated Vata.

s35. What is the role of meditation in Dinacharya?

a) To promote concentration and reduce stress

b) To enhance physical strength

c) To support digestion

d) To remove toxins

Answer: a) To promote concentration and reduce stress

Explanation: Meditation calms the mind, improves focus, and fosters emotional balance, complementing the physical health benefits of Dinacharya.

36. What is the purpose of gargling (Kavala or Gandusha) with oil or water?

a) Strengthens teeth and gums

b) Prevents bad breath

c) Improves oral hygiene and detoxifies the mouth

d) All of the above

Answer: d) All of the above

Explanation: Gargling strengthens oral tissues, prevents dental issues, and removes toxins, contributing to overall oral and systemic health.

37. Why is bathing (Snana) considered essential in Dinacharya?

a) To enhance appearance

b) To cleanse the body and calm the mind

c) To induce hunger

d) To balance Pitta Dosha only

Answer: b) To cleanse the body and calm the mind

Explanation: Bathing removes impurities, relaxes the mind, and promotes alertness, ensuring hygiene and mental rejuvenation.

38. What time of day is exercise NOT recommended?

a) Early morning

b) Evening

c) Night

d) Late afternoon

Answer: c) Night

Explanation: Exercise at night can overstimulate the body and disturb sleep patterns. It is best done in the morning or early evening.

39. Why is it advised to avoid sleeping during the day in Dinacharya?

a) It increases Kapha and causes sluggishness

b) It disrupts the natural biological clock

c) It leads to indigestion

d) All of the above

Answer: d) All of the above

Explanation: Sleeping during the day disrupts metabolism, accumulates Kapha, and causes indigestion, leading to lethargy and imbalance.

40. Why is avoiding excessive talking or shouting recommended in daily routine?

a) To conserve energy and maintain mental peace

b) To prevent throat disorders

c) To avoid disturbing others

d) Both a and b

Answer: d) Both a and b

Explanation: Limiting unnecessary talking prevents stress on vocal cords, conserves energy, and maintains mental calmness.

41. What is the ideal method of applying oil for head massage (Shiro Abhyanga)?

a) Light strokes

b) Vigorous rubbing

c) Circular movements on the scalp

d) Applying randomly

Answer: c) Circular movements on the scalp

Explanation: Circular movements stimulate hair follicles, improve blood flow, and relax the mind.

42. Why is moderate eating recommended in Ayurveda?

a) To avoid weight gain

b) To maintain digestive fire (Agni) and prevent Ama (toxins) formation

c) To improve immunity

d) Both b and c

Answer: d) Both b and c

Explanation: Overeating weakens Agni and leads to Ama, causing indigestion and diseases. Moderate eating supports digestion and immunity.

43. What is the Ayurvedic guideline for brushing teeth?

a) Use herbal powders or twigs from specific trees

b) Use chemical-based toothpaste

c) Brush only once a week

d) Use metallic toothbrushes

Answer: a) Use herbal powders or twigs from specific trees

Explanation: Twigs from neem, babool, or licorice have antibacterial and strengthening properties beneficial for oral health.

44. Which Dosha predominates during the morning hours (6:00–10:00 AM)?

a) Vata

b) Pitta

c) Kapha

d) None

Answer: c) Kapha

Explanation: Morning hours are dominated by Kapha, which is heavy and sluggish, requiring stimulation through light routines and exercise.

---

45. Which activity in Dinacharya supports emotional stability?

a) Meditation

b) Vigorous exercise

c) Eating heavy food

d) Sleeping excessively

Answer: a) Meditation

Explanation: Meditation calms the mind, improves emotional regulation, and fosters mental clarity.

---

46. What is the ideal time for oil massage (Abhyanga)?

a) Before exercise

b) After bathing

c) Before sleeping

d) During mealtime

Answer: a) Before exercise

Explanation: Abhyanga is performed before exercise to relax muscles, improve circulation, and prepare the body for physical activity. It also helps in detoxification by loosening toxins for elimination.

---

47. Which herbal twigs are most commonly used for brushing teeth in Ayurveda?

a) Neem, Babool, and Licorice

b) Bamboo and Coconut

c) Banyan and Palm

d) Eucalyptus and Pine

Answer: a) Neem, Babool, and Licorice

Explanation: Twigs of Neem, Babool, and Licorice are antimicrobial, anti-inflammatory, and beneficial for gum health. These herbs strengthen teeth, prevent decay, and maintain oral hygiene.

---

48. What is the significance of using cold water for bathing in the morning?

a) It enhances Pitta

b) It reduces body temperature and stimulates circulation

c) It weakens the immune system

d) It is only for summer

Answer: b) It reduces body temperature and stimulates circulation

Explanation: Bathing with cold water in the morning is refreshing and balances Pitta Dosha by cooling the body. It also improves blood circulation and energizes the body.

49. What is the main cause of Kapha aggravation according to Dinacharya?

a) Skipping meals

b) Sleeping during the day

c) Overexposure to the sun

d) Eating spicy food

Answer: b) Sleeping during the day

Explanation: Daytime sleep slows metabolism, increases heaviness, and accumulates Kapha in the body, leading to sluggishness and potential weight gain.

50. Why should meals be eaten at regular intervals in Ayurveda?

a) To regulate hunger

b) To maintain proper digestion and Agni (digestive fire)

c) To save time

d) To promote Kapha

Answer: b) To maintain proper digestion and Agni (digestive fire)

Explanation: Regular meals help keep the digestive fire active and balanced, ensuring that food is properly digested without forming toxins (Ama).

51. What does Ayurveda recommend avoiding immediately after a meal?

a) Drinking warm water

b) Sleeping or lying down

c) Walking slowly

d) Relaxing in a seated position

Answer: b) Sleeping or lying down

Explanation: Sleeping after a meal slows down digestion, increases Kapha, and causes indigestion. Ayurveda advises light activities like a short walk to aid digestion.

---

52. What is the effect of performing yoga or pranayama in the morning?

a) It increases Vata

b) It calms the mind and energizes the body

c) It promotes lethargy

d) It imbalances Pitta

Answer: b) It calms the mind and energizes the body

Explanation: Morning yoga and pranayama enhance oxygenation, stimulate the nervous system, and balance the Doshas, leading to mental clarity and physical vigor.

---

53. What is the significance of waking up during *Brahma Muhurta* (early morning)?

a) It balances Kapha Dosha

b) It enhances spiritual and mental clarity

c) It promotes indigestion

d) It increases laziness

Answer: b) It enhances spiritual and mental clarity

Explanation: *Brahma Muhurta* (approximately 90 minutes before sunrise) is considered an ideal time for spiritual practices, meditation, and mental focus due to the calm environment and heightened awareness.

---

54. How does tongue scraping benefit the body?

a) Removes toxins and stimulates taste buds

b) Cleans the throat

c) Balances Kapha only

d) Improves Pitta Dosha

Answer: a) Removes toxins and stimulates taste buds

Explanation: Tongue scraping clears Ama (toxins) accumulated on the tongue, improves oral hygiene, and enhances taste perception, which indirectly aids digestion.

---

55. Why should hair oiling (Shiro Abhyanga) be avoided in cold weather without proper care?

a) It increases Kapha and leads to cold or sinus issues if not washed properly

b) It dries the scalp

c) It aggravates Pitta

d) It causes hair loss

Answer: a) It increases Kapha and leads to cold or sinus issues if not washed properly

Explanation: Leaving oil in the hair for prolonged periods, especially in cold weather, may aggravate Kapha, leading to sinus congestion and other related issues.

---

56. What is the primary benefit of proper sleep as per Dinacharya?

a) It increases Kapha only

b) It restores bodily tissues and mental health

c) It weakens Agni

d) It makes the body heavier

Answer: b) It restores bodily tissues and mental health

Explanation: Proper sleep balances the Doshas, promotes tissue repair (Dhatu formation), and refreshes the mind, ensuring overall health and vitality.

---

57. How is Vata imbalance avoided during travel as per Dinacharya?

a) By eating heavy meals

b) By applying oil to the skin before travel

c) By staying awake at night

d) By drinking iced water

Answer: b) By applying oil to the skin before travel

Explanation: Oil application nourishes and lubricates the skin, which helps pacify the dryness and lightness associated with Vata, making it a beneficial practice during travel.

---

58. Why is seasonal cleansing (Ritucharya) mentioned alongside Dinacharya?

a) To make the daily routine more interesting

b) To remove seasonal toxins and adapt to climatic changes

c) To promote Kapha imbalance

d) To eliminate the need for daily routines

Answer: b) To remove seasonal toxins and adapt to climatic changes

Explanation: Seasonal cleansing helps the body transition smoothly between seasons, preventing Dosha imbalances and maintaining harmony with the environment.

---

59. Which sense organ benefits most from regular Nasya (nasal therapy)?

a) Eyes

b) Ears

c) Nose and brain

d) Skin

Answer: c) Nose and brain

Explanation: Nasya clears nasal passages, enhances respiratory function, and nourishes the brain by supporting sensory and cognitive health.

---

60. What type of food should be avoided during breakfast according to Dinacharya?

a) Light and warm foods

b) Heavy and oily foods

c) Fresh fruits and nuts

d) Cooked vegetables

Answer: b) Heavy and oily foods

Explanation: Heavy and oily foods during breakfast slow digestion and increase Kapha, leading to lethargy and sluggishness throughout the day.

---

61. What is the effect of maintaining a consistent wake-up and sleep schedule?

a) Promotes irregular bowel movements

b) Balances circadian rhythms and improves digestion

c) Increases stress levels

d) Imbalances Vata Dosha

Answer: b) Balances circadian rhythms and improves digestion

Explanation: Consistency in sleep and wake times supports the body's biological clock, enhancing digestion, metabolism, and overall vitality.

62. What is the recommended daily duration for meditation or mindfulness practice?

a) 1–2 minutes

b) 15–30 minutes

c) 2–3 hours

d) No specific recommendation

Answer: b) 15–30 minutes

Explanation: Ayurveda suggests 15–30 minutes of meditation to calm the mind, reduce stress, and improve focus, which complements physical health.

अष्टांग हृदयम, सूत्रस्थान, अध्याय 2 - दिनचर्या (दैनिक दिनचर्या)

दिनचर्या अध्याय में दैनिक जीवन को संतुलित और स्वस्थ बनाए रखने के लिए उचित आहार, जीवनशैली, और दिनचर्या के नियम दिए गए हैं। इसमें वायु, पित्त और कफ जैसे दोषों के संतुलन को बनाए रखने पर जोर दिया गया है।

---

1. ब्रह्म मुहूर्त जागरण (सुबह जल्दी उठना):

सूत्र:

ब्रह्ममुहूर्ते उत्तिष्ठेत् स्वस्थो रक्षार्थमायुषः।

(Brahmamuhurte uttiṣṭhet svastho rakṣārtham āyuṣaḥ.)

अनुवाद:

स्वस्थ व्यक्ति को आयु की रक्षा के लिए ब्रह्म मुहूर्त (सूर्योदय से लगभग 45-60 मिनट पहले) उठना चाहिए।

व्याख्या:

- सुबह उठने का समय शरीर के प्राकृतिक जैविक चक्र के अनुसार होता है।

- यह समय मानसिक और शारीरिक शुद्धता, अध्ययन और ध्यान के लिए सबसे अच्छा माना गया है।

---

2. शौच (मल-मूत्र विसर्जन):

सूत्र:

नित्यमेव मलमूत्रे शुद्धे विधिवत् कुर्यात्।

अनुवाद:

प्रतिदिन उचित समय पर मल-मूत्र का विसर्जन करना स्वास्थ्य के लिए आवश्यक है।

व्याख्या:

- सुबह मल-मूत्र त्याग शरीर के अपशिष्ट पदार्थों को निकालकर वात, पित्त, और कफ को संतुलित करता है।

- कब्ज या अनियमितता दोष असंतुलन का कारण बन सकती है।

---

3. दंतधावन (दांतों की सफाई):

सूत्र:

कट्वम्लतिक्तरसैः कषायैरदन्तपाकिनः।

(*Kaṭvamlatikta-rasaiḥ kaṣāyairadantapākinaḥ.*)

अनुवाद:

कड़वे, कसैले, और तिक्त रस वाले द्रव्यों से दांतों की सफाई करनी चाहिए।

व्याख्या:

- नीम, बबूल, और अन्य जड़ी-बूटियों की टहनियों से दांत साफ करना लाभकारी होता है।

- इससे मुंह की स्वच्छता बनी रहती है और मसूड़ों के रोग दूर होते हैं।

---

4. जीवा निरलेखन (जीभ की सफाई):

सूत्र:

जिह्वा निरलेखनं कुर्यात्, दोषान् निर्मलती सदा।

अनुवाद:

जीभ को स्क्रैप (साफ) करना दोषों को संतुलित रखता है और शरीर को स्वच्छ बनाता है।

व्याख्या:

- जीभ पर जमा मैल पाचन तंत्र को प्रभावित करता है।

- तांबे या चांदी की स्क्रैपर से जीभ साफ करने की सलाह दी जाती है।

---

5. अभ्यंग (तेल मालिश):

सूत्र:

स्नेहनं शिरसः कान्तिं स्नेहनं च त्वचां शुभम्।

(*Snehanaṃ śirasaḥ kāntiṃ snehanaṃ ca tvacāṃ śubham.*)

अनुवाद:

तेल मालिश सिर और त्वचा को पोषण देती है और सौंदर्य व कांति को बढ़ाती है।

व्याख्या:

- नियमित अभ्यंग (तेल मालिश) से वात दोष शांत होता है।

- यह त्वचा को मुलायम बनाता है, रक्त प्रवाह में सुधार करता है, और मांसपेशियों को सशक्त करता है।

---

6. व्यायाम (शारीरिक अभ्यास):

सूत्र:

अर्धशक्त्या निशेवेत व्यायामं।

(Ardhaśaktyā niṣeveta vyāyāmam.)

अनुवाद:

व्यायाम अपनी क्षमता के आधे भाग तक करना चाहिए।

व्याख्या:

- व्यायाम शरीर को मजबूत करता है, पाचन अग्नि को बढ़ाता है, और दोषों को संतुलित करता है।

- अत्यधिक व्यायाम करने से वायु दोष बढ़ सकता है।

---

7. स्नान (नहाना):

सूत्र:

स्नानं ह्लादं कृतं दर्प पापक्लमकषायपम्।

(Snānaṃ hlādaṃ kṛtaṃ darpaṃ pāpaklamakaṣāyapam.)

अनुवाद:

स्नान से शरीर और मन को प्रसन्नता, ऊर्जा, और शुद्धि मिलती है।

व्याख्या:

- नहाने से त्वचा की स्वच्छता, रक्त परिसंचरण, और दोषों का संतुलन होता है।

- अत्यधिक ठंडे या गर्म पानी से नहाने से बचना चाहिए।

---

8. आहार सेवन (भोजन के नियम):

सूत्र:

हितं मितं च योग्यं च आहारं सेवेत।

(*Hitaṃ mitaṃ ca yogyaṃ ca āhāraṃ seveta.*)

अनुवाद:

स्वस्थ रहने के लिए उचित, संतुलित, और सुपाच्य भोजन करना चाहिए।

व्याख्या:

- भोजन का समय नियमित होना चाहिए।

- अत्यधिक ठंडा, गर्म, या मसालेदार भोजन दोष असंतुलन का कारण बन सकता है।

९. निद्रा (सोने का नियम):

सूत्र:

युक्तस्वप्नो युक्तचित्तः।

(*Yukta-svapno yukta-cittaḥ.*)

अनुवाद:

उचित समय और मात्रा में सोने से मन और शरीर का संतुलन बना रहता है।

व्याख्या:

- रात में जल्दी सोना और सुबह जल्दी उठना आदर्श माना गया है।

- दिन में सोने से कफ दोष बढ़ सकता है, और अनिद्रा से वात दोष प्रभावित होता है।

---

१०. नित्य धर्म पालन:

सूत्र:

धर्मं सेवेत्रित्यं, सत्संगः शुभम्।

अनुवाद:

नित्य धार्मिक और नैतिक कर्तव्यों का पालन करना चाहिए।

व्याख्या:

- सकारात्मक सोच, आध्यात्मिकता, और सत्संग मानसिक शांति प्रदान करता है।

- इससे मनोविकार और भावनात्मक असंतुलन दूर होते हैं।

दिनचर्या के लाभ:

- दोष संतुलन बनाए रखना (*वात, पित्त, कफ*)।

- पाचन अग्नि और प्रतिरोधक क्षमता को बढ़ाना।

- दीर्घायु, स्वास्थ्य और मानसिक शांति प्राप्त करना।

- मौसमी बीमारियों और विकारों से बचाव।